Tish & Pish

How to be of a speakingness like Stephen Fry

A delicious collection of sumptuous gorgeosities

by Stewart Ferris

summersdale

TISH AND PISH

Summersdale Publishers Ltd
46 West Street
Chichester
West Sussex
PO19 1RP
UK

www.summersdale.com

ISBN 1 84024 466 6

Printed and bound in Great Britain.

for Stephen Fry

Contents

Introduction

This book is not about Stephen Fry. It is about taking his delightful way of using the English language and applying it to phrases from everyday life in a parody of a foreign language phrasebook.

These phrases are not intended to reflect the character of Stephen Fry, nor should it be inferred that he has ever uttered such phrases. Indeed, he may never wish to speak the word arrangements presented in this book and his reputation as a bright and articulate speaker may be all the more solid for such abstemiousness.

The first version of each phrase is written in 'normal' English; the second version represents a style of English that is inspired by an overall perception of Stephen Fry's writings, speech and acting roles.

English is a versatile language, so let's have some spankingly good fun with it…

BASIC PHRASES

Oh, well.	**Heigh-ho.**
Anyway, so.	**Tinkerty-tonk.**
Yes.	**Indeed may it be so.**
No.	**I am entirely of a disagreeingness.**
Thank you.	**I am indebted and pleasured by you in equal measure.**
Please.	**Pleasure me.**
Goodbye.	**Toodle-pip.**
Pardon?	**There is too much fur in my ear: would a recapitulation be too much of a supplication?**
Excuse me.	**Discharge me from the love muscle of blame into the moist receptacle of absolution.**
Blimey.	**Tish and pish.**
How are you?	**May I enquire as to whether you are in receipt of a state of bodily wellness?**

GREETINGS

Hello.	**Good hello.**
What's up?	**What of an upwardsness is?**
Oh no, not you again.	**Tish and pish, has the restraining order already expired?**
Can I help you at all?	**Is there some manner in which my acquired skills or the sum total of my knowledge or even the kinetic capabilities of my muscular frame can assist you as you journey through this ticklish life?**
Yo!	**Felicitations!**
Pleased to meet you.	**I tingle in your presence.**
Good evening.	**May the period of duskiness titillate and fulfil you.**
Hi, allow me to introduce myself.	**Greetings, pleasure me with permission to present myself to you for evaluation as a potential friend, lover or colleague.**
Happy holidays!	**Merry non-specific ecclesiastical or secular platitudes for the season.**

EXPRESSIONS OF DISPLEASURE

I disagree. **Fiddlesticks and
humgudgeon.**

Nonsense. **Tummy rubbish.**

Ouch! **My previous state of
harmonious well-being
has been impaired by a
discomfiture resulting from
a curt but vexatious and
detrimental external
impact upon my tegument.**

Oh no! **It is impossible to express
within the constraints of
the English lexicon the
longitude, fathomage,
latitude and stature of my
dismay.**

Idiots! **Hare-brained
pithecanthropoids!**

THE WEATHER

This isn't the rainy season. Britain is always like this.

This is not the equinox characterised by excessive dampness, precipitation and golfing umbrellas. *Britannia* **rules the waves because she is thusly deluged** *in perpetuum.*

I hear that there's a hosepipe ban because it's only rained for three hundred and twenty days this year.

If my headly appendages do not deceive me, the rubber *calamus* **is under interdiction because we have only been in a moistened state for sixteen score planetary revolutions in the current solar circumnavigation.**

This kind of weather is called bracing. It's meant to be good for you.

This genus of climactic condition has a nomenclature referring to its ability to aid stiffness. Such fortifying stimulation is said to be spankingly beneficial thereto.

PEDANTRY

What do you mean, 'England have been knocked out of the World Cup'? How many Englands are we talking about?

What is your intended phrasal signification when you ejaculate the words 'England have been knocked out of the World Cup'? What precise quantity of lands of hope and gloriousness are we verbally tossing up?

No this is not going 'to really be' a nice day if you use split infinitives like that.

On the contrary, any peachyness that might be applicable to this solar ascendancy will be negated by your verbal vulgarity if you persist with split infinitives such as, ugh, it pains me to say it, 'to really be' (*sic* – I think I will be).

PEDANTRY

When you say you 'ain't got no bananas left' then logically you do have some bananas left by reason of a double negative making a positive. So I'd like two bananas, please.

According to your avowal, you are in possession of an unspecified plural number of the yellow phallic-shaped fruit of the tree-like herb of the genus Musa by reason of your double negative making a positive. Therefore I would like to purchase two of the aforementioned comfort-shaped trouser-enhancements.

What do you mean, 'three alternatives'? How can there be more than one alternative?

What am I expected to infer from your bizarre proclamation that we have 'three alternatives'? *Alter*, Latin for 'the other of two'. It is not possible for there to be more than one alternative to something. Your sentence is therefore meaningless and you are an imbecile.

PEDANTRY

How can it be 'fairly unique'? Either it is or is not unique.

Your method of transmission of information is as foul, depraved and ghastly as the English language can provide, for the word 'unique' cannot, by definition, be qualified by an adverb in the way that your linguistic knowledge can be qualified by many adverbs including beastly, unhealthy and amoral.

How can you have an 'amount of people'? Will you put them all through a blender and pile up the remains?

I am of a curiousness to see a visual representation of your description of an 'amount of people'. People come in single units, not portions thereof, and can therefore be counted in whole numbers. The only way to obtain an amount of people is to blend, mash and scoop them into a bulging amassment.

PEDANTRY

What do you mean, we will 'de-plane momentarily'? Are we all meant to jump back on immediately afterwards?

I cannot comprehend your intended meaning when the word 'momentarily' is suffixed to the non-existent term 'de-plane'. If by the latter you are trying in your own vulgar manner to describe the act of egress from this flying machine then by combining it with 'momentarily' you imply that such an act of disembarkation is not only temporary, but pointlessly ephemeral.

How can my book be 'a roller-coaster ride that blossoms into a rare flower'?

In what mannerism can my oeuvre be a spiralling locomotive thrill journey at a park for unimaginative families and simultaneously a colourful herbage on the endangered species list? Metaphors are like chocolate and caviar: they should never be mixed.

PEDANTRY

Describing it as 'the biggest ever of all time' is tautologous. Please exercise economy and restraint in your language.

Erecting a verbal canvas and covering it with such audacious hyperbolic splashes as 'the biggest ever of all time' is pleonastic, grandiloquent, bombastic, tautological, tautologous, circumlocutory, periphrastic, flowery, prolix, fustian, garrulous, repetitious, repetitive, magniloquent, long-winded, tedious and tortuous. Pleasure me with the employment of frugality, abnegation, temperance, abridgement, moderation, abstemiousness, parcity, concision, pithiness and succinctness in your parlance.

PEDANTRY

I understand that the sign says 'do not walk on the grass', but I was running, not walking.

It is not beyond my comprehension that the implication of this sanitised form of street graffiti in brass and wood is that perambulation upon the lawn is frowned upon most severely. However I was, like your nose, *en courant* and therefore my kineticism does not fall within the limited definition of your banishment.

ETIQUETTE

It's bad manners to put your hand down there before we've been introduced.

It would be considered contrary to the accepted norms of this society for you to put your hand within the crevice of my lower attire precedent to our formal introduction by a third party.

Where I come from we normally use the other entrance.

In my country of origin it is customary for a first-time visitor to enter via the front door; the back door being reserved for those with whom one is more intimately ensconced.

I'll put it away if it offends you.

If it should turn out to be the case that your sensibilities are too fragile to cope with the sight presented hereto I will take all necessary actions to screen your field of vision.

ETIQUETTE

A man should be seen and not smelled.

A gentleman should ensure that his bodily odour is neutral in its output such as can be attained through regular contact with water and soap, and it would be altogether incorrect to be of an invisibleness.

Of course I would like to come out on a date with you, but who will be our chaperone?

It is beyond question that I am desirous of taking you out for sundry spooning purposes with the implied subtextual anticipation that the success of such an occasion and subsequent occasions of that ilk may lead to an eventual espousement, but who will accompany us to ensure that no immoral rumpy-pumpy can taint our reputations?

Forgive my old-fashioned sexism, but ladies first.

I may be a bit of a fuddy-duddy sexy, but gentlewomen must be of a prioritisement.

ETIQUETTE

I would offer you some money, but I feel it would be bad manners to open my rather fat wallet in front of a homeless person.

Your request puts me in something of a quandary for as much as I would gain satisfaction from being of a charitableness and donating a small sum of money thereto, I am fortunate in having sufficient good taste to know that it would be vulgar of me to reveal and open my bulging reticule in front of a penniless person of no fixed abode.

I'm not sure that it's decent for you to be showing so much ankle.

Vile and degenerate whore! Cover that bare ankle from public view otherwise I shall have no recourse but to send you to the workhouse for fallen women.

ETIQUETTE

If you talk any louder into that mobile phone they'll be able to hear you from here anyway.

If the volume at which you are of a speakingness into that portable contraption of telephonic communication were to increase in decibelature by even a modest degree then I would expect that the person or persons with whom you are so publicly conversing would be able to hear you without the requirement for a cellular radio infrastructure to transmit your digitally encoded voice signal.

In the bathroom

What are you doing in my bathroom?

Pleasure me with an explication of your presence here in my defecation, urination and cleansing chamber.

Please open the window next time.

On any subsequently comparable defecatory occasion I would be grateful if you would transfer the fenestration from being of an impermeableness to being of an otherwise nature.

I'll just be a couple more minutes.

The completion of my movements and the subsequent clean-up operation will require no more than two minutes.

Can I borrow some reading material?

Pleasure me with the temporary lendition of printed literature suitable for voracious linguistic devourment in a ten minute burst.

In the bathroom

There must be something wrong with these scales.	**By means of logical deduction, to wit the excessively high numeration indicated on the readout of this weighing machine, there must be a malfunction.**
I thought it was a number one but it turned into a number two.	**I was anticipating a bodily excretion of the first prime number but the net result of my toiletary session was a solid commonly referred to by the great unwashed as the first even number.**
Hurry up in there – I'm touching cloth.	**Accelerate your expulsion, ablution, or masturbation therewithin – my faecal sausage is starting to make friends with my undergarments.**
Where's the bog?	**Could you assist me by pointing out the most appropriate route to the, ahem, smallest pavilion?**

In the bathroom

I wouldn't go in there if I were you. Not for ten minutes, at least.

The explosion of aroma that just took place has a probable half-life of approximately ten minutes, therefore I would not recommend ingress to the affected zone unless you are partial to the whiff of last evening's chicken tikka massala.

I bathe every week, without fail, whether I need to or not.

I submerge my naked corpulence in a tin container coated with a thin layer of white enamel and filled with water at a temperature of thirty-five degrees Centigrade and a solution of synthetic chemicals which when combined with the aforementioned heated water creates a luxuriance of bubbleage hebdomadally irrespective of whether I am in receipt of a thusly necessitousness.

ON THE PHONE

I spell my name with a 'p'.

I am of a spellingness my name with a 'p'-ness.

No I don't require any double glazing but thank you so much for calling and while you're on the phone I wonder if I could just read to you the first draft of my novel that I've just completed? Hello?

My spouseless fenestration is sufficient for my needs, but I am appreciative of your telephonic contact and whilst we are engaged in this impromptu dialogue perhaps I could read to you the first draftington-bertie of my novel? Good hello?

Do you not understand English?

I would not expect a call centre operative to be conversant with Old English, but when I quote phrases to you in Middle English I expect to be understood.

How's the weather in India today?

How is the combination of such meteorological variables as barometric pressure, temperature, wind velocity, and moistness in the Indian subcontinent today?

ON THE PHONE

I can't hear you very well.

Are you holding the telephone receiver in an upside-down manner or do you have your noodle immersed in a pail of water?

I'm sorry, I think I dialled the wrong number. Can I chat to you anyway?

I am penitent to my unworthy knees for the unforgivable erroneousness of my dialage. Can I confabulate with you anyway, if you don't find the prospect too unhygienic?

Do I mind holding? Holding what?

Do I mind being of a holdingness? What precisely would you like me to be of a holdingness?

Hello? Is that the speaking clock?

Good hello? Is that the instrument of time measurement which has the capacity for parleyosity?

ON THE PHONE

You want to sell me what? Hold the line while I go out and buy a pen to write it down.

What did you want to exchange with me for some of my hard-earned units of remuneration? Maintain your grasp on the telephony wire while I journey to the most proximate population centre to procure an implement of scripture with which to inscribe your words of wisdom.

EATING OUT

I like to eat out.

There is nothing more gently arousing than acquiring mastery of one's fellow man, having him at one's beck and call for an hour or two, catering to one's every whim, simply by entering his establishment and partaking of a main course.

Waiter, there's a spider on my chips.

Steward, this dish appears somewhat more arachnidan than was indicated on the list of victuals.

I write restaurant reviews, you know, so don't be stingy with the ketchup.

I craft written appraisals of eating establishments, in case you are not thusly cognisant, therefore I suggest that liberal dollops are in order when it comes to matters catsuppian.

EATING OUT

My usual table please, Maître d'. It's that one. By the window.

Pleasure me with my habitual dining console, Master Dennis. It is the one located of a thuslyness. Proximate to the fenestration.

Send my compliments to the chef. He needs some encouragement by the looks of this dish.

Communicate my panegyrics to the long-haired youth in the chequered trousers who works in your kitchen even though he appears not to have completed his BTEC course in basic cooking. He could benefit from some inspiritment judging by the appearance of this entrée.

It said fish fingers on the menu. Plural. Where's my other finger?

The fare of comestibles stated, in a legally binding manner, the phalangic representations of cold-blooded, Piscean vertebrates. Being designative of more than one. Pleasure me with the location of my other digit?

EATING OUT

Your chef works that microwave as if it were part of him.

Your cheffing personage operates that kitchen appliance that produces heat by generating an electromagnetic wave which is absorbed by water molecules in the food as if it were an extension of himself, although the erection of any such extension would be subject, of course, to the necessary planning consents.

Waiter, you call that garlic bread? I could hardly taste the garlic. Kiss me and I'll show you.

Steward, you denominate that as a leavened flour and yeast slice flavoured with the clove of the herb *Allium sativum*? No detection of the presence of any particles of such a bulb was made by my eager and inquisitive tongue. I can prove it by inserting my mouth muscle into your primary facial orifice.

Eating out

Waiter, I've got a bit of a dirty knife. Would you kindly take it and insert it into the washer-upper for me?

Steward, my scimitar is mildly befouled. Pleasure me with its removal from my person and insert it into your gentleman or lady colleague whose employment responsibilities are predominantly concerned with the cleansing of such lancets.

At the doctor's

Doctor, doctor, it hurts when I laugh. Can I have some painkillers or a Little and Large *DVD to make sure I don't laugh?*

Physicians both, I experience a state of unpleasantness when I chortle, titter and gaffaw. Pleasure me with a prescription of appropriate pharmaceutical remedies or a Digital Versatile Disc of *Infinitesimal and Immense* to ensure the mirth reflex cannot be activated.

Is it really necessary to hold them while I cough?

Is it truly *de rigeur* to cup them in your warm and gentle palms while I expel phlegm, mucus and pieces of breakfast from my spongy, compound sacular organs of oxygen extraction?

You're just a quack.

You are but a mountebank and a charlatan, and you are reminiscent of my favourite Chinese dish.

At the dentist's

Is it going to have to come out?

Will it be requisite for it to become extra-oral?

I find it hard to get into the gaps.

I lack the necessary crevice-entering skills.

I like your ceiling.

I approve of and enjoy viewing from this reclined position your covering of British Gypsum boards and off-white emulsion paint that marks the upper limit of this torture chamber.

Can I have a general anaesthetic to take away with me?

Would it be beyond the realms of appropriateness for me to request a spare portion of blissful oblivion potion in a doggy bag?

I wish I'd looked after my teeth.

I am retrospectively desirous that I had paid more attention to the message within the weighty poetry of Pam Ayres.

At the dentist's

Ouch! That hurts like crazy!

I feel I can no longer refrain from uttering an almost involuntary expression of discomfort. That which you are doing inside my cavity must be cessated forthwith if I am to avoid leakage from my tear ducts.

Do you have any mouthwash? Only your breath stinks a bit.

Do you have in this establishment any quantities of that green liquid that was apparently invented as a floor cleaner and was subsequently discovered to have beneficial effects when taken orally (provided one remembers to spit, not swallow)? The reason that I thusly ask is that the gaseous by-products of your lung-based oxygenation process smell like rotten eggs.

At the dentist's

What did you find in my mouth? Oh, that: I wondered where it had gone.

What foreign object did you pluck from my astonished jaws? Your revelation has registered with me in a memory-provoking manner, for that object was one of which the location had for some time occupied my thoughts and mystified me.

Aren't we supposed to make smalltalk before you enter me?

Are we not supposed to converse in a manner that avoids topics that pertain to any significance, preferring to focus instead on such worthless trivialities as the meteorological situation, my means of journification and sundry sports events to which we may or may not have been witness? I understand that such a technique is commonly employed as a means of relaxing the two parties in dialogue, and should continue for a sufficient length of time for such a calming of nerves to occur prior to the insertion into my body of a part of yours.

At the dentist's

The pain starts in my tooth, but it runs all the way down to my inner thigh. Could you take a look?

The unpleasant sensation commences in my diseased dental protrusion, but its regular jogging route takes it all the way down to my private groinal zone. As part of your professional investigation into my symptoms I consider it necessary for you to feast your eyes thereupon.

At the Post Office

Can I send a telegram?

Can I send a telecommunicationogrammaticus?

Would you lick these for me? My tongue is reserved for one person only.

Would you be so goodly kind as to pass the moist organ in your mouth over these? I prefer to reserve my tonguing for a singularly fortuitous personage.

Could you ask E.R.N.I.E. to check my Premium Bond numbers?

Could you enquire as to whether your rather clever Rlectronic Random Number Indicator Equipment can review the numbers of my bond of superior characteristics?

I'd like a licence to kill, please.

I am desirous to be in a state of procurement of an extermination dispensation, pleasure me.

AT THE POST OFFICE

Oi, I was next!

If you'd studied the Kendall Classification of Queuing Systems you would realise that the Poisson Markovian method would favour the immediate obligement of my prerogative.

How big is your PO box?

What is the cubic capacity of your mail receptacle?

The delivery of this letter may not be special to you but it's special to me.

The deliverance of this manuscripted communication is of far greater consequence than can ever be dreamt of in your philosophy.

I'd like two Penny Blacks please.

My gratitude will flow torrentially in your direction if you could service me with a mating pair of the low denominational stampages of the tint that reflects no light.

AT THE POST OFFICE

I presume a first class stamp entitles me to the use of a first class lounge?

I postulate that a stamp of the premier class will entitulate me to a session in the facilities of that ilkington?

At the cinema

Please stop talking. I can't hear my own popcorn crunching.

Pleasure me with an arrestment of the audible drivel that is pouring from your facial orifice. I am unable to register the mellifluous tones of my exploded kernels of corn being masticated.

No, I can't sit any lower in the seat. If you don't stop complaining I shall put on a hat.

Regrettably it is beyond my spinal compression capacity to diminish my seated height. If you continue to lament your bad fortune in sharing this electric cinema with me I will have no option other than to place a topper upon my head.

British cinema is the finest in the world. Apart from a couple of other countries where they do it a little better.

Britannian electric kinematography is unequalled globally. With the exception of a brace of other kingdoms in which the phenomenon is consummated in an ameliorated manner.

At the cinema

Excuse me. Sorry.
Let me squeeze past.
Weak bladder.

Discharge me from the love muscle of blame into the moist receptacle of absolution. Observe my sincere compunction. Permit me to compress my body against some of the less interesting parts of yours as I pass by. My distensible membranous vesicle is somewhat decrepit and unreliable.

AT THE SUPERMARKET

This market really is super, don't you think?

This large grocery establishment is certainly superior in many ways, are you not thusly of a cognisanceness?

Can you lend me a pound for the trolley?

Is it within your physical, mental and pecuniary capabilities to provide me with an interest-free short-term loan of one British remunerative unit in coinage form for the purpose of releasing a wire-framed shopping chariot from its shackles?

No, I don't have a loyalty card.

I have no loyalty to this establishment: my loyalty is to my spouse and Her Majesty, and such loyalty occupies no space in my wallet.

Is this all the caviar you have?

Does this represent the entirety of your stock of egg-laden fish ovaries?

At the supermarket

Why can't I bring my dog into the shop? He's cleaner than a guide dog – at least I can see if he makes a mess and clean it up.

Furnish me with a valid reason as to the whyness that I cannot enter my canine chum into your establishment? The aforementioned beast is, by logical deduction, less likely to infest your aisles with doggy-dirt and other undesirables because I have the visual apparatus necessary to see such abominations and to initiate a course of action that would result in its cleanage.

There's a grammatical error on this list of ingredients, so could I have a discount please?

I have detected a syntactical misdemeanour on this tabulation of component foodstuffs and chemical additives, therefore I consider it justifiable to demand that a reduced level of fiduciary exchange be implemented in order to pleasure me.

AT THE SUPERMARKET

Before I pay for my shopping, perhaps you would do me the honour of letting me read to you a draft of my new novel? I'm sure those queuing behind me won't mind.

Precedent to the settlement of my account for the sundry comestibles, liquids, dishwasher tablets and generously proportioned prophylactics in my four-wheeled chariot, perchance you would honour me with the listenage of the most recent draft of my new novel? I have certainty that the shuffling hordes forming a linear pattern behind me will not object to such an experience of cultural edification.

Where can I find your value beans?

Where are the pleasantly-priced pulses of a locatedness?

THE ARTS

I felt that the Orange Prize winner deserved more than a piece of fruit.

In my excogitation, the estimable vanquisher of the guerdon that lies within the portion of the visible spectrum between red and yellow warranted something in excess of the ripened ovary of a seed-bearing plant.

If the history books are written by life's winners, who is writing the cookery books?

If the chronicles of times when all this was just fields are inscribed by those who have achieved a state of accomplishment, who is penning the monographs of comestible concoction?

I enjoyed this book from cover to cover. One day I should read the insides.

I pleasured myself with this opus from flap to flap. At an indeterminate point along the future time axis I will undertake a literary engorgement of its innermost titillations.

THE ARTS

Do you have a copy of the Yellow Pages*? I found it mentioned in this book about fly fishing by J R Hartley.*

Are you in possession of an ectype of a masterful work entitled *Yellow Pages*? I happened thereupon in this oeuvre about angling *de mouche* by J R Hartley.

I didn't enjoy that book: the writing was too verbose.

The gratification I anticipated from that literary tome utterly failed to lick me in the right places: the manuscript consistently employed protracted phrases when succinction would have been of a preferableness.

I've been attending life drawing classes for weeks. It's about time I started sketching something.

In recent weeks I have entered myself regularly in colloquia for the delineation of the denuded human embodiment. The present moment is appropriate for the commencement of a doodle.

THE ARTS

No wonder so many of the First World War poets were killed. They would have stood a better chance holding a gun instead of a pencil.

It could not be further from a matter of startlement that a prodigious proportion of versifiers in the Titanic Tussle kicked the wire-handled, cylindrical vessel for the transportation of liquid. The probability of an elongation of their vitality would have increased had they carried ordnance instead of a lead-based implement of scripture.

I thought his Madame Twinkie was magnificent.

In my considered opinion, his reprisal of the classic role of Madame Twinkie was commanding, majestic and sumptuous – a veritably Larry Olivieresque performance oozing with Johnny Gielgudian magnetism, Ralphy Richardsonian stature and Ray Winstonian sexuality.

THE ARTS

There's nothing like the roar of the greasepaint and the smell of the crowds.

Nothing can equate to the rambunctious vociferation of the maquillage and the malodorous issuance of the multitude.

I miss the old days of rep, changing in toilets, sleeping on floors and living on pennies. That was the life: simple, happy days. Now what's happened to my buttock masseur?

How one yearns for the bygone days of repertory theatre, sheathing oneself in dramatic apparel in the little boy's room (one so vividly remembers his look of awe and wonderment), taking forty winks on the linoleum and existing on a pittance. Thusly was life golden: uncomplicated, exultant times. Heigh-ho, has anyone seen my posterior pummeler?

BUYING A CAR

I don't need a parcel shelf, but a bookshelf would be handy.

My requisites do not extend to an out-thrust for the purpose of supporting my hefty package, however a protuberance appropriate for a mixed selection of bound opuscules, folios and weightier tomes would be of some beneficence.

Does the sound system play seventy-eights?

Is the intra-vehicular gramophone system capable of the playback of discs requisite of a spinnage at seventy-eight revolutions per minute?

Do you have one with more headroom?

Is it possible for you to provide me with a vehicular model comparable to this one but with the added benefit that one doesn't need to pilot it with one's head protruding from the sunshine-roof?

BUYING A CAR

Where do you insert the starting handle?

Into which greased orifice does one attempt the ingress of the stiffened baton designed for getting things moving on a chillsome first blush of a cock crow?

Can I have the seats finished in tweed?

Is there an option for the reclining davenports to be gowned in finest gabardine?

Does it come with a chauffeur or will I need to learn to drive?

Is a becapped technical operative a standard feature with this device or will I need to undertake a rigorous training programme in order to become qualified to pilot the thing myself?

BUYING A CAR

If I wanted to stop in a lay-by and write a novel, does this car have an onboard dictionary to help me with the big words?

Should a situation arise involving my velocital arrestment at a suitably stiffened *épaule* for the purpose of inscribing a fictional opus, does the vehicle possess lexicographical facilities that would assist me in finding appropriate polysyllabic expressions?

Purchasing Electronics

I'd like to buy an iPod please.

Kindly permit me to procure a wireless instrument of magnetic sound registration.

This little thing can take photos and record video? Next you'll be telling me it can make phonecalls too!

This diminutive contraption has the wherewithal to enregister photographic representations and moving pictures? Consequent to this astonishing revelation I would not be in a condition of ghasted flabber if you were to claim that one can also use it in connection with telephonic voice communications.

How do they fit all the valves into such a small box?

How can the little men in white coats squeeze their enormous vacuum tubes into such tight crevices?

Purchasing Electronics

What's the point in texting from a mobile phone when there's a perfectly functional postal service able to deliver messages within just a few days?

Why insult the English language with the vulgarity that is an abbreviated textual communication from a wireless telephone apparatus when the postal service, operating with all the oiled smoothness of a massaged *derrière*, has the capacity to be of a deliveringness the written word within the exiguous period of a few rotations of the earth's axis?

If I have to press this button then it's not automatic, is it? Automatic, from 'automatos'. I find it hard to believe your marketing people don't have even the tiniest smattering of Greek!

If one has to depress this thrust-action switch then the device ipso facto is not of an automaticness. Automaticness, from 'automatosness'. I find it singularly impossible to believe your vendition experts can perform their tasks without an iota of knowledge of the verbal communication system developed by the Ancient Greeks!

Purchasing electronics

Of course I understand that it's a digital camera: how else would I operate it other than with my fingers?

It's hardly beyond my intellectual capacity to comprehend that this photographic apparatus is digital in operation: in what manner would I activate this machinery other than with the digits of my forelimb?

Do you have any in Bakelite?

Do you have in stock any of these in encasements of black synthetic resins?

Does it get Radio 4?

Is it of a receivingness the Home Service?

Never mind Grand Theft Auto, *can I play chess with it?*

Never mind the electronic software programme that mimics the deplorable phenomenon of taking vehicles without the permission (whether written or verbal) of their owners or lawful keepers, can this device dally in the distraction of chess?

COMPUTERS

Do you have an e-mail address?

Is there a domicile situated along the cyber-thoroughfare at which you can be reached via electro-mail?

I seem to be stuck in a porn loop.

When one window is of a closing-downness, another one is of an opening-upness, thus dragging me roughly through the seedier backstreets of Cyber-upon-Tweed.

When I press this button the cup holder slides inside the computer and spills coffee over me.

Accompaniment to my squishing of this outthrust, the chalice stabilising protrusion retracts inside the electronic arithmetic engine and spurts warm liquid across my palpitating chest.

COMPUTERS

Hello computer. How are you? Hello? This thing doesn't work.

Good hello, logical data processor. May I enquire as to whether you are in receipt of a state of bodily wellness? Good hello? This contraption is in receipt of a state of considerable enfeebleness.

I upgraded its RAM and put in a new hard drive and still it doesn't love me.

I ameliorated its Random Access Memory and installed a neoteric Winchester drive of adamantine nature despite which the ungrateful beast continues to hold me in the lowest regard.

POP MUSIC

Wouldn't it be nicer if they all wore suits and ties?	**The portage of uniform three-piece suits with silk neck decorations by all the members of this pop combo would ameliorate immeasurably my viewing and listening experience thereof.**
I say, that chap sings well considering he could use a haircut.	**How is it possible for that pop star gentleman to exude what is undeniably a moderately catchy – almost sticky – melodiousness when his cranial follicular length is significantly greater in measurement than that which is acceptable for someone testicularly equipped?**
What they need is a good spell in the army.	**The one thing that would nip in the bud the vivacity, optimism and charismatic energy of this rock quartet is two score months of National Service.**

POP MUSIC

Could you turn the volume down, please?	**Pleasure me with a decibelature diminution.**
Whatever happened to those nice Beatles lads? They seemed promising.	**Did that rather pleasant, cheeky groupage performing under the amusing trademark of 'The Beatles' ever achieve the modest commercial and musical success that they deserved? I was certain that they stood a chance of making a living from their guitar and harmonica act.**
Gosh – that one doesn't even have his shirt on.	**Tish and pish – one of those male performers seems to be under the blatantly erroneous assumption that it is morally and legally acceptable to appear sans Ascot and Henley shirt from Burlington Arcade before an audience some of whose members may not be in possession of as strong a stomach as my own.**

POP MUSIC

Was that a song? I thought it was just feedback.

Have I just experienced the listenage of a three-minute ballad? I was of the opinion that the vibrations in my aural canal were the regenerations of sounds picked up by a transducer and output through an amplifier in an infinite loop.

It might sound better if we stood back a little – a couple of miles perhaps?

Our appreciation of these audible frequencies might be ameliorated if we repositioned ourselves relative to the source thereof – optimally at a distance of about sixty-three thousand inches.

Funny, I never came across this group on Radio 4.

Curiously, my almost incessant listenership of the Home Service never encountered this collection of musical miscreants.

POP MUSIC

I considered a career in pop music myself, but unfortunately I'm a trained musician.

At that roundabout of life that we all come to, stalling our engines as we nervously look for signs to guide us to a suitable career, I considered taking the M40 to pop stardom, but regrettably my Penny Farthing of traditional musical training was not permitted to use a motorway and would have been forced to take the B4016 to Didcot.

CLASSICAL MUSIC

I have a very cool classical collection. Some of the works are less than a hundred years old.

My assemblage of mechanical recordings of classical oeuvres is meritorious and unobjectionable. A small, indeterminate portion thereof has yet to celebrate its centenary.

I love Beethoven. Any film with dogs in it gets my vote.

I am in receipt of a state of fond admiration for Beethoven. Any moving picture of which the principal cast member is canine and which puts itself up for democratic election to any level of administrative office can be sure of my support in the ballot box.

That music provoked many passions in me, not all of them entirely legal.

That sequence of melodies, harmonies and rhythms launched my concupiscence in multifarious directions, some of which may be contrary to the laws of decency, morality and nature.

CLASSICAL MUSIC

I liked the bit near the end, but they were too heavy with the ukulele.

The penultimate movement moved me sufficiently that my trousers required adjustment, but my pantaloonical modification would have been greater had the ukulele soloist succumbed to a rather sudden and debilitating illness.

It's been three hundred years since this music was written: that means it's actually older than Rod Stewart.

This musical work was composed in the period of such world-changing events as the decline of the Ottoman Empire, the rise of the Ching Dynasty, and the introduction of counter-balanced box sash windows, making it even more superannuated than Rod Stewart.

CLASSICAL MUSIC

I tried to take up the clarinet and I couldn't sit down for a week.

I made an attempt to assimilate the single reed air tube into my curriculum vitae with the result that I was unable to let my gluteus maximus make contact with any hard object for the duration of a seven day calendar period.

They say the cello sounds like a human voice: well I can't play or sing and when I attempt to do so my voice does indeed sound like my cello playing.

Personages of indeterminate quantity and identity have commented that the large, firm instrument that is plucked or stroked between the legs emits an audible excretion that is comparable to the *vox humanus*: my ability to pluck or stroke in the aforementioned music-creating manner is so ear-mashingly dire that it does indeed create a cacophony comparable to that generated by my attempts to conduct my tongue and throat in a tuneful direction.

CLASSICAL MUSIC

This is sheet music? Why has someone covered it with little squiggles?

This is a symbolic representation of the tonal and rhythmic intricacies of musical composition? Furnish me with an answer as to the whyness that someone has apparently sprinkled the paper with diagrams of spermatozoa?

Spoon-playing seems to be a bit of a dying art.

The making of enjoyable rhythmic audibleness with mouth-size metallic shallow bowls on sticks is regrettably a cultural form of entertainment that is in terminal decline.

CELEBRITY PARTIES

Which celebrity list are you on? In your case perhaps we need a longer alphabet?

Which alphabetical category of luminaries is blessed with your presence? A more elaborate system of representative language characters might be utilitous in your case.

Your presence here suggests that the word 'celebrity' has the most malleable definition in the English language.

Your ubiety at this gathering of well-known dignitaries implies that the term 'celebrity' possesses the most supple and flexible elucidation in the Anglo-Saxon tongue.

FLIRTATIOUS PHRASES

My skin tingles when I'm near you.

My corns are itching with a libidinous concupiscence in your presence.

If I said you had a beautiful body would you hold it against me?

If I verbally articulated the splendour and unblemished beauty of your physicality, would it in any way prejudice your sentiments with regard to the individual who habitually refers to himself by the perpendicular pronoun?

Hi, I'm a weatherman, and I've been admiring your warm front.

Good morrow. I happen to be in the meteorological profession and am somewhat enamoured of your temperate zones.

Let's get something straight between us.

What could be frothier than to have something rectilinial hereto of an in-betweenness?

FLIRTATIOUS PHRASES

Hi, I'm a postman, so you can rely on me to deliver a large package.

How do you do? As a messenger of the written word you can rest assured that I will do my level best to ensure prompt and accurate deliverance of sundry parcels, no matter what their mass and density (provided any one package weighs less than thirty-three kilos, that loadage being the maximum I am permitted to lift according to regulations).

Hi, I'm a doctor. What's your appendix doing tonight? I'd love to take it out.

Accostments, I spent seven inebriated years at medical school and am therefore sufficiently qualified in the healing arts to propose this evening that I whip out your appendage.

FLIRTATIOUS PHRASES

I can read you like a book. I bet you're great between the covers.

Your forehead appears to have about seventy-thousand words imprinted thereupon. I'd hazard that you are accomplished in the rumpy-pumpy department.

Hi, I'm here on a computer date, but the computer hasn't shown up.

Good hello, my presence here was determined by an electronic arithmetic engine which for reasons unfathomable to a mere human has deigned it necessary to be elsewhere tonight. Hello? Where have you gone?

TELLING JOKES

There was an Englishman, a Scotsman and an Irishman…

There was a member of one ethnic group, a member of another ethnic group, and a third person from an ethnic group which was often perceived as comical by the first two. The first one said something innocuous, as did the second. But the third said something that in isolation would be innocuous but in the context of what the others had said and taking into account his ethnic stereotype, was capable of generating amusement.

What do you get if you cross one ordinary item with another ordinary item? Something amusing.

As a consequentiality of genetically assimilating one object with something of an otherwiseness, of what might you be in receipt? A phenomenon stimulating the bodily reflex that is the physical manifestation of mirth.

TELLING JOKES

Why did the chicken cross the road?

What was the intent of the *gallus domesticus* in traversing the asphalt artery?

How many of a particular stereotype of person does it take to change a lightbulb?

What math unit correctly indicates the sum of personages of a stereotypical nature requisite for the changeosity of an incandescent lamp?

I was walking down the street the other day...

I was perambulating down an unspecified public thoroughfare during an equally unspecified twenty-four hour period of earth rotation...

I'm not saying my mother-in-law's fat, but...

Far be it for me to postulate on the corporealitiness of the immediate genetic female ancestor of my spouse, but...

TELLING JOKES

How does an Essex girl do something on a sex related topic?	**In what particular manner does a debutante from the home county of Essex perform an indeterminate copulatory act?**
Doctor, doctor, I think my illness might be a good set-up for your punchline.	**Physician, physician, I consider that which ails me to be the archetypal Ernie Wise to your Eric Morecambe.**
I say, I say, I say…	**I am of a sayingness, I of a sayingness am, I saying am of an ofness…**
Knock knock…	**An audible collision between the joint of the metacarpals and phalanges and a hinged, wooden entrance structure, an audible collision between the joint of the metacarpals and phalanges and a hinged, wooden entrance structure…**

ON CAMPUS

No, I'm not a professor. I just dress like one.	**No, I profess that I am a professor not, but I confess my apparel does tend to point in a thusly direction.**
Which course are you studying?	**Which tripos elements have you embraced for this academic annus?**
Do you have any courses that are a little more challenging?	**I finished that degree before breaking my fast today. Could you furnish me with something with which to occupy myself this afternoon?**
I'd like to take part in University Challenge.	**I am desirous of making a complete arse of myself on the televisor.**
I thought that new nightclub was awful.	**That neoteric nocturnal establishment must be the closest one can get to a purgatorial underworld on earth without actually studying at Oxford.**

ON CAMPUS

Can I cadge a loan of your pen?

Would it be possible to negotiate a non fiscal, temporary borrowance of your implement of scripture?

I want all students to wear denim tomorrow to show their support for my cause.

My earnest desire is that all the other university undergraduates will be of a wearingness on the morrow a coarse twilled cloth such as is to be found in jeans and other borderline immoral forms of youthful clothage in order to display their advocation of my ill-considered and naïve pet obsession.

I'm under so much pressure: my ten week summer holiday is ages away and I have four hours of lectures to go to this week.

I am under an oppressive condition of mental distress caused by the eternity I must wait before the commencement of my deca-hebdomadal series of holy days and the unreasonableness of having to attend four hours of lecturisations this week.

ON CAMPUS

Hey, why don't we steal that traffic cone? I bet no students have ever done that before!

I venture to suggest that we perform a misappropriation of that traffic cone, on the grounds that the execution of the aforementioned proposal will provide an original and fresh reason for the local residents to feel rankled by students.

Of course a degree in Assyriology is going to stand me in good stead when it comes to getting a job.

My chances of successfully bagging a worthy and satisfying jobbage cannot fail to be enhanced by my Assyriological knowledge.

EMPLOYMENT

It's always been my ambition to work in communications. Do all postmen get their own bike?

My cherished desire since pre-pubescence has been to find gainful employment in the transmission of information. Does each man of letters benefit from his own velocipede?

Do any of your jobs come with bigger desks?

Do any of your remunerative engagements provide me with a bureau that is greater in magditudinalness?

Working hours? I was hoping it could be measured in working minutes.

Working time intervals measured as one twenty-fourth of an earth day? I held a desire, accompanied with an unjustifiably confident expectation of its fulfilment, that it could be quantitively standardised in units of working minutes.

EMPLOYMENT

Please don't be put off by the fact that I can write grammatically correct English; I still think I'd make an excellent journalist.

I will pleasure you on the condition that your prejudices are not awakened by the alarm clock of my impeccable English grammar; contrary to perceived ill-wisdom, I possess the potential to excel as a scribe for the sewage outlet of mankind that is the printed news medium.

I think you'll find my C.V. is in order. It should be for the money I paid.

I hazard a guesstimation that your opinion of my curriculum vitae will be of a positiveness. It thusly ought so to be considering it cost twenty pounds.

I wasn't unemployed during those years: I was resting.

It would not be correct to deduce from my inactivity during the passage of those years that I was not in a state of gainful employment as it was a necessary period of revivification.

EMPLOYMENT

Would I be allowed to wear a cravat with the uniform?

Is there a judicial stipulation that would prevent me from donning a particularly manlysome fabric scarf around my neck to complement my pre-supplied homogenous outfit of employment?

Will someone be showing me how to use a one of those computer thingies?

Will an unspecified personage demonstrate the utilisation of one of those electronic arithmetic engine doobries?

I've always wanted to do whatever this job is.

I have, since time immemorial, been desirous of filling my remaining working days on this earth with whatever this jobbage may be of a beingness.

EMPLOYMENT

I was thinking of taking next year off as a holiday. That wouldn't be a problem, would it?

I do have a small number of holy days planned, amounting to less than four hundreds. I trust that would not in any way prejudice my chances of obtaining gainful employment herewith?

FILMMAKING

I'm making a film about posh people in the twenties, so would you mind removing all of your television aerials and cars from this street?

Through the channel of my directorial hands I intend to beget a moving picture about hoity-toity types in the roaring decade that followed the end of the First World Fisticuffs, and as a direct result of which begatment I require the ousting of your roof-mounted metallic apparatus for the receiving of televisual signals and your motor chariots from this thoroughfare.

I wrote the screenplay myself, so I'm confident that you'll find no spelling errors.

I quilled this screenplay singlehandedly (for there were other things I preferred to be of a doingness with my other metacarpus), therefore I can with aplomb assure you that no deviations from that which is considered correct lexical positioning will tarnish your otherwise shiny outlook.

FILMMAKING

Kenneth, darling, please make an effort to learn your lines.

Kenneth, oh fondly-favoured one, pleasure me with some degree of exertion in the direction of the remembrance of your lineage.

Lights! Camera! Action!

Electromagnetic radiation within the wavelength range of 4,000 to 7,700 angstroms! A box with a lens at one end that takes twenty-four photographic images per second which when viewed in rapid succession create the illusion of movement! A transition from a state of doing nothing (other than the natural processes of one's internal organs necessary for continued survival plus some minor muscular corrections to help with balance and comfort) to a state of being of a doingness something which in this instance clearly relates to the noble art of acting!

FILMMAKING

Can we try that again? My scarf got caught in the sprockets.

Is there any possibility that we could endeavour to reproduce that scene anew? My woolly neck-warmer became ensprocketed in the moving picture apparatus.

Gaffer! Grip! Runner! Someone please help me with these trousers!

Young boy charged with sticking cables to the ground so that we don't trip over them and end up foul of the current health and safety at work legislation! Another young boy charged with setting camera apparatus on tripods so that the final effect of simulated movement appears smooth as a baby's bib after washing! Much younger boy charged with doing anything us adults want him to do despite not getting remuneration for his efforts! Will any of the aforementioned boys pleasure me with some assistance in my trouser department?

FILMMAKING

Please hurry up and get this scene in the can – I'm on Jonathan Ross *later.*

Pleasure me with an acceleration of your motions in order that this scene can be of a completedness before I squeeze the hand of Jonathan Ross.

Would you like to be an extra?

Are you desirous of being in receipt of a small part?

That was excellent but we forgot to turn on the cameras. So everyone get their clothes off again and we'll try once more.

That effort was of a superior quality but the moving picture machine was set to a state of inactivity. If all persons present could pleasure me with their redisrobing we can reproduce our previous endeavours.

That's a wrap.

That of a terminatedness is.

AT WIMBLEDON

I'd like a portion of strawberries with cream.

My object of longing is a serving of sufficient quantity of the red, fleshy, edible fruits of the perennial herbs of the genus Fragaria to satiate one adult plus enough spare of the aforementioned pulpy berries to allow for a socially-acceptable form of robbery known as food tasting by one's friends without prior permission, covered with a liberal splash of the surface accumulation of yellow fatty deposits to be found in unhomogenised milk.

I don't care if this is the Duchess's seat – I was here first.

It matters to me not one jot if these buttocks belong to the Duchess – the law of England states very clearly that 'finders are of a keepingness, losers are of a weepingness'.

AT WIMBLEDON

What time is Sir Cliff Richard on Centre Court?

When will I be able to pleasure myself with the viewing of the traditional visitation of Britain's foremost Christmas cash-in pop star on the Centre Court?

It was better when they had those wooden racquets.

The game of tennis was ameliorated in the past by the use of those instruments of hittingness made from the wood of recycled trees and the guts of recycled cats.

I apologise for the smell: I queued all night for a chance to see Fred Perry.

I submit my remorsefulness regarding my malodourousness: for the confused and demented hope of viewing Fred Perry I stood in line long past the witching hour at the Wimbledon gate.

At Wimbledon

Was that chalk dust or did some cocaine fall out of his nose?

Do you think that spray of a white powdery substance was a result of the impact of a tennis sphere upon a line in the grass indicated by white calcium deposits created by long-dead organisms, or did a euphoria-inducing pharmaceutical erupt from his nasal passage?

Where are the Wombles?

Can you inform me as to the whereabouts of the children's characters popularised by television in the seventies who are said to recycle rubbish on a scale that would have a negligible beneficial impact on the health of the environment, and taking into account the merchandise produced in their name over many decades for ungrateful little darlings who have since grown up and thrown their unwanted toys into landfill sites must have had overall a highly damaging effect on the planet?

AT WIMBLEDON

I love coming to Wimbledon. It has such a great shopping centre.

Wimbledon has a tug that makes me come time and again. It is in possession of a centre of excellence in the field of commercial agglomerations.

FOOTBALL

The referee's a blind
!#!

The adjudicator is a visually-impaired canal in a female mammal that leads from the uterus to the external orifice opening into the vestibule between the labia minora!

We are the champions!

We, and by the pronoun of the first person plural I actually mean the team to which I and numerous others dedicate our waking moments and our wage packets rather than to any group of which I am actually a member, are without doubt at our absolute zenith: we are superior in sundry sports-related qualities such as teamwork, fitness and firm-thighs; we are more successful than similar groupings of players who form the rival clubs; and our wife-beating and drink-driving exploits are a role model for the young generation!

FOOTBALL

Send him off!

Instruct him in the strongest possible terms to vacate the field of play forthwith!

He was offside!

He was subject to football's most obscure rule, one which is reputedly beyond the comprehension of any female (albeit because it bores them so much that they fall into a coma before hearing the end of the explanation) but equally one which many males do not fully understand either because they act as if their brains have slid down into their testicles.

That was never a foul!

The incident that resulted in the flashing of a yellow card was not at any point in its execution something to be considered in contravention of the rules of this rather base form of mass entertainment.

FOOTBALL

He's faking!

He appears to have withdrawn from the football match and has begun painting in oils a strikingly accurate and convincing copy of one of Leonardo da Vinci's most intriguing works, *The Virgin of the Rocks* (the Musée du Louvre version, of course).

We're one point away from relegation. I'm not worried, though; if we go down I'll just support another team.

Our team's poor performance over the course of the last season makes excessively likely its banishment to a place of exile where the tendrils of television sponsorship cannot reach. This potential state of affairs concerns me not, however, for if it should come to pass I will avoid disappointment by transferring my allegiance to another aggregation of firm-thighed lads.

FOOTBALL

Like ninety per cent of their supporters, I've never actually been to Manchester.

In common with the preponderance of other fanatics who claim as their own this international business posing as a football club, I have never actually set foot within the parish boundary of Manchester.

Football is not something I admit to watching except when there's a World Cup on. Then it becomes socially acceptable amongst those who know how to use a knife and fork.

I deny any and all associations with the merriment of ball-kicking for periods of four years, renouncing such dignity only during the tournament for which the prize is the Global Mug. The vulgar passion I can then exude will have temporary immunity from badinage amongst the users of implements of cutlery.

PETS

What a magnificent pussy. May I give it a stroke?

Your fine feline friend impresses me. May I rupture a blood vessel to create partial damage to its brain so that it becomes dizzy and incontinent?

I think I can see your tortoise head peeping out.

The closure of the nylon teeth that provide instant access to your trouser zone would be an advisable way of shading your rather shy and cuddly-looking pet.

I've heard it said you keep a dragon in there. Oh, doesn't she like being called that?

The local ill-founded windmill of rumour has it that you maintain in captivity a draconine enshacklement. Tish, does not her of intramural habitation appreciate that nomenclature?

Do I like rabbits? Yes, but I'm not really hungry right now.

Do I harbour lagamorphic desires? Indeedy, but I've already sated my appetition.

PETS

I didn't know you had a horse. What was it like?

I was not cognisant that you either were once (or remain) in ownership of an equine beast, assuming the concept of 'ownership' can really be said to extend to living entities, or, if I may lower the tone somewhat by adopting the baser meaning of the word 'had', that you enjoyed caballine carnality at some point. Of course, were you of Gallic origin, I would push my enquiry in the direction of matters culinary. Whichever of the meanings applies thereto, was it of an enjoyableness?

You have a parrot? And there was I thinking you'd never get a bird.

You are in possession of a feathered animal of the genus volucrine? My presupposition that your avian-adverse status would stretch henceforth *ad nauseum* is clearly and happily piffle.

PETS

They say pet owners grow to look like their pets. I'm glad I bought a snake.

There are those who, presumably having nothing better to say, make pointless comments about pets and their looky-likey masters. It pleasures me that my animal purchase was ophidian.

How much is that doggy in the window? The one with the waggly tail.

What quantity and denomination of promissory notes would be required to effect the purchase of the full legal title to that canine beast behind the pet shop fenestration? The one with the symptoms of psychological damage from having been incarcerated and lonely during its formative months.

Please don't allow your dog to pee on my shoe.

Pleasure me with the cessation of canine urination, whether for purposes of bladder easement or for territorial claimage, on my leather foot encasement.

CLICHÉS

A bird in the hand is worth two in the bush.

A feathered aerial or flightless dinosaur descendant in the phalanges possesses the same utilitarian value as two feathered aerial or flightless dinosaur descendants in the follicular growth of the lower hypogastric region.

There's no place like home.

There exists no edifice, community or geographic area that can be said to compare favourably with the place at which one habitually resides.

The grass is always greener on the other side.

The green herbage with narrow leaves that makes a useful ground covering for gardens and public spaces is unfailingly perceived to be a more green shade of green on a piece of property adjoining one's own slightly less green patch.

CLICHÉS

*He's worth his
weight in gold.*

**His value to society
measured both in monetary
and moral dimensions is
equal to the fiscal result of
comparing his body mass to
an equivalent mass of a soft
and malleable, corrosion-
resistant yellowish element
that can be found in alluvial
deposits and ascertaining the
value thereof.**

*Every cloud has a
silver lining.*

**Every visible collection
of fluffy, floating water
particles possesses a surface
layer of a lustrous, pliable
metallic element of the
Atomic number forty-seven.**

As blind as a bat.

**As visually impaired as a
nocturnal flying mammal,
only without the
compensation of a naturally-
evolved radar system that is
anyhow far more effective at
locating insects and cave
walls than ocular equipment.**

Clichés

Are you a man or a mouse?	**Are you of the genus hominine or are you of the genus that is likely to send sitcom actresses screaming and standing on a chair?**
At the crack of dawn.	**Situated between the yawning crevices of the early ante meridiem.**
You haven't got a leg to stand on.	**You are not in possession of a locomotive stick on which to place your not inconsiderable weight.**
You can't make an omelette without breaking eggs.	**You, or any other personage here present or *in absentia*, do not have a smidgen of a tad of a Liechtenstein of a morsel of a fragment of a dash of a pittance of an iota of a scintilla of a hope of manufacturing an egg-based pancake-style breakfast dish without violently smashing unfertilised female gametes.**

FAMOUS QUOTATIONS

'Never in the field of human conflict was so much owed by so many to so few.' (Winston Churchill)

'Never in the bailiwick of hominine disputation were so many lashings of gorgeousness owed by so many to so piddling a number.'

'To be, or not to be: that is the question.' (William Shakespeare)

'To of a beingness be or not to of a beingness be: that is the split infinitive version of the interrogative rhetorical phrase.'

'This is the sort of English up with which I will not put.' (Winston Churchill)

'This is the sort of English up with which I will not of a puttingness be.'

'That's one small step for man; one giant leap for mankind.' (Neil Armstrong)

'That is one fluffy steppage for man; one not inconsiderable cavort for mankindness.'

FAMOUS QUOTATIONS

'I was working on the proof of one of my poems all the morning, and took out a comma. In the afternoon I put it back again.' (Oscar Wilde)

'I was toiling on an unfinished draftington of one of my poetic inscribances throughout the ante meridiem, the net result of which was the removal of a minor item of punctuation used in setting the pace and rhythm of a sentence. Post meridiem I returned the aforementioned punctuational symbol to whence it came.'

'Ask not what your country can do for you – ask what you can do for your country.' (John F. Kennedy)

'Refrain from putting forward an enquiry on the subject of any benefits you can claim from your nation state – propose instead an enquiry directed at yourself on the subject of what you can be of a doingness theretofore.'

TRAVELLING

I'm allergic to plastic cutlery and holidaymakers so please could you upgrade me?

I suffer from adverse bodily reactions, including, but not limited to, rashes, spots, itching and weeping, when I come into contact with bendy, non-metallic eating implements and travelling members of the lower echelons of society. Therefore pleasure me with a seat on this aircraft that is several times more valuable than that for which I have actually paid.

I like to educate people I meet when travelling.

The true felicity of peregrination comes in the opportunity it presents to edify the ignorami who can be found in towns everywhere littering the streets with their split infinitives, mixed metaphors and crisp packets.

TRAVELLING

Please stop kicking the back of my seat.	**Pleasure me with a cessation of the kickingness of the *derrière* of my buttock-support device.**
Oi, taxi!	**Forgive my shouting in the street in this rather vulgar manner, but I should like to reserve the usagenosity of your taximeter cabriolet for a journey to... oh, fiddlesticks, someone else has beaten me thereto.**
I never like to visit a town that doesn't have a bookshop: I fear the uncultured locals might eat me.	**The visitation of a population centre that exists without the facility of a store for the vendition of bound monographs gives me the willies for there is a disturbing possibility that its unhousetrained inhabitants might cover me in ketchup and vinegar and microwave me.**

TRAVELLING

Travelling is good for the soul but bad for the soles.

Being in a state of transition from one location to one of an otherwiseness is beneficial to the essential spark at the centre of one's humanity whilst at the same time creating an undesirable level of weariness on the leather or rubber bases of one's pedal claddings.

Oh no – I've missed my train!

Fiddlesticks and humgudgeon, my tardiness has resulted in a locomotive departure *sans moi*!

HOLIDAYS

Can you direct me to the easyJet first class lounge?

Can you furnish me with verbal instructions as to the optimum route via which I can arrive at the first class drinkery and rest environment in which I can hide away from the plebeian hordes whilst sipping cocktails in anticipation of my easyJet flight?

What do you mean you don't speak Latin? This is Rome, isn't it?

Are you in earnest when you claim an inability to articulate verbally the Latin communication system? Is this Rome, or is it of an otherwiseness?

Why would I want to drive on the right?

What could possibly possess me to be desirous of piloting my internal combustion-powered vehicle on the starboard side of the highway?

Holidays

According to my trusty 1937 atlas, your country is still part of the Empire.

Your country is printed in a noble pink hue in my authoritative pre-war bound collection of maps, indicating that it continues to be part of our imperial sovereignty.

Please boil your hands before you touch me.

Pleasure me by cleansing your hands in water at or approaching three hundred and seventy-three degrees on the Kelvin scale precedent to any bodily contact you may attempt herewith.

Where can I buy a copy of The Times?

At what commercial edifice, preferably within a moderate perambulatory distance of my present location, can I be of a purchasingness a copy of *The Times* newspaper?

HOLIDAYS

I'd like a pint of ale, a steak and kidney pie and a packet of pork scratchings por favor, señor.

For my luncheon I would like you to serve me a unit of liquid volume used in the imperial measurement system equivalent to approximately half of your queer litre things of Old Thumper, a baked pastry filled with sundry cow parts including its urine cleansing organ and a packet of pig by-products, if you will pleasure me young man.

Please respect my personal space.

Pleasure me with some deferential regard for my small but comfortable three dimensional geographic area.

This is a toilet? I was going to take a shower in here.

You classify this as a porcelain fixture for the receipt of urine and faecal deposits? I was going to be of a cleansingness myself therewithin by standing under a fine spray of warm water.

HOLIDAYS

I have the utmost regard for these French savages.

I possess the maximum permissible non-sexual feelings towards the backward, barbaric, uncivilised horse-eating primitives who inhabit the land of Gaul.

AT THE BEACH

Would you please rub some cream onto my skin? There's a tub of Devonshire clotted in the cool box.

Would you pleasure me with the caressment of a dense, milky-style liquid onto my largest bodily organ? Within the firkin in which the air temperature is significantly lower than the external ambience can be located a vial of Devonshire coronary.

I didn't know this was going to be a nudist beach. Wait here while I fetch my camera.

The unattired condition of the inhabitants of this sand strip between the endless ocean and the endless car park was not a phenomenon that could have been predicted by any logical thought processes based on my life experiences to this date. Do not move from this position of longitude and latitude (although movement in time is permitted so long as it is in a forwardly direction) until I return with my Box Brownie.

AT THE BEACH

Can you tell me where the changing rooms are?

In order to enjoy immersing myself in the almost freezing cesspit that is our seawater, I intend following the perverse tradition of wearing fewer garments than I would in warmer environments. Is it within your capacity to furnish me with the location of the bathing machines?

Can you help me get the knots out of my hanky?

Can you assist me with the removal of the intertwinings of my square piece of white cotton weave that despite being engrained with sundry nasal emissions has been affixed to the top of my head for the duration of my embeachment?

My wind-break appears to have blown away.

It is apparent that my roofless tent-like structure designed for shielding me from the merciless winds that ravage the southern English coastline during July and August was insufficiently bedded to the pebble beach and is now flying to France.

AT THE BEACH

It's rather hot on this beach. I think I should loosen my tie.

Being situated on this accumulation of waterside sand deposits is far hotter than the temperature at which a person can be said to be comfortable. After having considered many potential solutions to this botheration, including the removal of myself from this place, I will resolve instead to slacken the knot in my neck cravat, thus enlarging the diameter of the silk ring and reducing the quantity of contact with my skin in order to allow greater circulation of air with the intended net result of a minor reduction in my body temperature and an equivalent increase in my level of gratification.

At the Beach

Why is everyone just sunbathing when they could be fossil-hunting?

I fail to understand the odylic force that makes personages lie on the sand in an attempt to obtain the colour-change effects of superficial radiation burns when there are shapely remnants of prehistoric organisms wedged cachés in certain rock strata in the adjacent cliffs that can be revealed with a simple hammer and chisel and a large sun hat.

I was water-skiing and I went off-piste. I'll pay for any damage to your garden.

During a recreational session involving my towage on flat sticks behind a small sail-less vessel I strayed from the traditional water-based route. The rectification of your vegetable patch and lawnage will be at my expense.

AT THE BEACH

Hey everyone – a shark! Oops, no, it's a bit of wood. Wait – it is a shark! No, maybe not.

Could I take the liberty of interrupting whatever my fellow beachites, one and all, may happen to be doing, in order to declare that I have spotted – in the sense of viewing rather than covering in spots of paint – a carnivorous fish of the Chondrichthian class (subclass Elasmobranch), with heterocercal caudal fins and nasty pointy teeth? Well roger me ragged with a rusty rod, contrary to my previous announcement which seems to have precipitated a mass panic and evacuation of the water, I now revise my statement of the discovery of the aforementioned fourteen-gilled beast to announce instead the flotation of a solid, fibrous-lignified substance of arborial origin. Arrest your sudden resumption of seaward migration – contrary to my

At the beach

contrarinous, my pre-
contrarial statement
regarding sharkage is now
to be considered a warning
worthy of heed and therefore
it seems likely that you are
all now fishfood. Although
when I consider the evidence
one more time, it cannot be
ruled out that we are
facing a situation of an
otherwiseness.

*I hate getting sand in
my novel. Should
have stayed in the
library, really.*

I am in receipt of a state of
negative pleasure when
ground silicate sedimentary
material with grain sizes of
between six hundredths of
a millimetre and two
millimetres in diameter find
their way into my printed
and bound monograph. Such
an unfortunate occurrence
could have been avoided had
I remained in the librarium.

In New York

You get the biggest and longest of everything here in New York.

It is possible to get one's hands upon the most girthsome and most ultimately satisfying of that of which one is desirous here in the freshly-created version of the Roman city of Eboracum.

I said 'brown bread', please. You find that amusing?

I merely requested 'brown bread' in reply to your solicitation as to the variety of leavened flour and yeast slice that would most appropriately accompany my *petit déjeuner*. Is there something about my suggested comestible that is a source of gaiety and mirth?

I don't like entering the Queens tunnel – I find it rather claustrophobic.

It gives me no pleasure to insert myself into the Queens deep passage at Midtown – I experience an irrational sense of panic and paranoia.

In New York

I just want my eggs fried. You decide on the specifics.

I am merely desirous that the metamorphic system employed in your kitchen to create edible ova should be to cook them over direct heat in hot oil or lard. The precise details, methodology and timings I am content to leave to your own wise judgement.

Apparently I am a legal alien here in the Big Apple.

According to the classification system operated by those wise chaps who govern the land that takes its name from Amerigo Vespucci, I am a being from another planet but with certain constitutional rights during my stay here in the capacious fruit of the deciduous tree *Malus pumila*.

I buy all of life's essentials in Christopher Street.

I procure in the Greenwich Village thoroughfare named after the wet-footed, third century Christian martyr all of the modern consumer items that make life so soft, warm and yielding.

In New York

I said Broadway and Forty-ninth Street, please, yellow cab driver. Do you not speak English or do you not know how to get there? Ah, it's both.

I requested that you pleasure me with a conveyance to a suitable stopping point at or near to the intersection of Broadway and Forty-ninth Street, operator of this taximeter cabriolet coloured with paint from the visible spectrum between orange and green reflecting light energy in wavelengths of about five hundred and eighty nanometers. Are you not orally cognisant of English or do you have no knowledge of the layout of the simplest-designed city in the world? Well tinkerty-tonk, a conjunction of the two appears to be prevalent.

In New York

I like to remain on the East Side of New York city. It makes me feel closer to home.

I harbour a preference for the exteriority of New York metropolis that faces the ascendant ball of refulgence. Thusly can be enhanced my sense of domiciliary proximation.

How clever of George Washington to have anticipated the size and prevalence of American cars when he built his bridge.

How sagacious of George Washington to have prognosticated with such penetrative skill the voluminosity and excessive quantity of SUVs and other monstrously unnecessary vehicular appendages that compensate inadequate American males when he erected his enormous span across the Hudson.

CURRENT AFFAIRS

I think women should be given the vote.

I am of the opine that the half of the population that is more reasonable and lighter in hue, sometimes known as the 'fairer sex', should have a say in the election, selection and erection of our governmental members.

Free Nelson Mandela!

Set at liberty from his incarceration for political agitations carried out so long ago that I can't recall what they were any more the man who has come to symbolise all that is wrong with the oppressive regime of which he is a victim, Nelson Mandela.

Apparently the world is warming up. It's nice to have a bit of good news.

As far as one can trust one's appendices of sensory input the mean temperature of the planet is rising. How cordial to be in receipt of cheering revelations.

CURRENT AFFAIRS

I like that Mr. Gladstone: his bag is very fetching.

My affableness extends warmly towards Mr. Gladstone: his behandled-container of leathery stiffness suitable for carrying a packed lunch, a small hat or the affairs of state within its hinged compartments is most teasing.

I hear they can put a man into space these days!

The grapevine that buzzes with the vibrations of a thousand rumours and ends in my organ of hearing informs me that our species now has the capacity to escape the shackles of gravity and to journey to the void beyond!

It's those Teddy boys that I worry about.

I succumb to a significant botheration when I reflect on the threat to our soceity's moral undergarments posed by those youths with their smart suits, combed hair and tendency to enjoy music.

CURRENT AFFAIRS

You don't hear much about the Communists these days. Perhaps it's time for another witch-hunt?

The communist domination of our paranoias that we used to enjoy seems to have melted away. I propose that the time is upon us to choose another aspect of philosophical idealism over which to lose sleep and to use as a basis for the persecution of intellectuals.

That President Carter floats my boat.

That President Carter enables the suspension on the meniscus of the water my navigable method of bodily transport.

I'm worried about the spread of ASBOs. You can develop horrible lung illnesses from that stuff.

I have an irrelevant and misguided worriment about the diffusion of ASBOs. One can come down with pneumoconiosis as a result of contact therewith.

FINANCE

I'm sorry, but it's impossible for me to know if I can spare ten pence for a cup of tea until my accountant has completed my tax affairs at the end of the financial year. If you'd care to contact me in writing at that time I'd be happy to consider your request.

Compunctious as I am of a beingness, any supererogatory aspect of my fiscal situation will only become apparent when my chartered bean-counter concludes his calculations in respect of my government tithes as one financial loop around the sun fades into the next. Any scribal approach in respect of your aforementioned request for fundingness vis-à-vis your proposed tea-purchasing project will thencely be given unabridged rumination.

Do you have change from a farthing?

Can you furnish me with a pecuniary remuneration by way of the difference between the value of the good or service that I am attempting to procure and an out of date, non-existent denomination of coinage?

Religion

I wanted the job of Pope, but apparently they were only taking applications from Catholics.

I was desirous of filling the Papal vacancy – however, I was denied access to this position due to a minor technicality relating to my non-membership of the *religare catholicus*.

I have a friend who goes to church religiously. He's a vicar, I think.

I am in the fortunate position of having a trusted acquaintance who punctiliously attends a proudly erectile edifice of spiritual reverence.
He is a devil-dodging plenipotentiary of Him upstairs, I faithfully believe.

POLITICS

I've given up voting: it seems that whoever you vote for, the politicians always win.

I have voluntarily relinquished my democratic privileges: from my perspective, whoever one selects at the ballot receptacle it would appear that the only victors are the sycophantic statesmen who form our honourable members.

I've already voted in Big Brother: *why do I have to vote in the General Election too?*

I have previously articulated my democratic voice in regard to the Mammoth Male Sibling: for what reason must I additionally take part in the Ubiquitous Referendum?

The British democratic system ensures that the country is always governed by a party for which more than sixty per cent of the electorate did not vote.

The Britannic system of governance by elected representatives unfailingly promotes to power a party which is deficient in the patronage of the majority of the great unwashed.

POLITICS

Is European Union a good idea or a bad idea? Well, it's certainly an idea.

Is the agglutination of the western peninsula of the Eurasian land mass an intellection that is of an agreeableness or of a disagreeableness? Indubitably it is an intellection.

Don't mention the war.

Refrain from the discharge, whether casual or subconscious, of verbal allusions to the multi-continental conflict.

LAW AND ORDER

Sending people to Australia used to be a punishment; now it's a treat. I wish they'd make up their minds.

Deportation to the antipodean colonies was once a legal instrument of retribution; now they are desirous that we spend our holy days therewithin. Nothing would fulfil me more than if a decision could be made once and for all and sundry as to whether Australia is suited only for matters penal or whether it is a bad place.

Hanging's too good for them.

Suspension by means of a rope around the neck tied to a gallows until the participant has asphyxiated is hardly a proper punishment: surely we need to take up a more rigid position against these people?

LAW AND ORDER

A clip round the ear would sort them out.

A fast and violent (but not causing permanent damage) blow to the side of the head using the back of the hand will suffice to be sorting them of an outness.

You caught me red-handed: looks like I could be going down.

Your Holmesian powers of deduction have resulted in my discovery mid-crime: the most likely sequence of events to result from such misfortune is one which will lead to a considerable stretch on my part.

Have you done porridge before, or is this your first time serving prison breakfasts?

Do you possess a personal history which includes a warm, oat-based meal often used for the breaking of fast and which is a synonym for a prison sentence, or are you a virgin employee of the penitentiary canteen?

Law and Order

Objection, m'lud!

I hereby state my opposition to a legal process or to a statement made by the opposing counsel which I consider to amount to improper evidence, m'colleague!

Does your haircut comply with European Union laws?

Is the style of your sprouting clump of carbon filaments complicit with the most recent legal postulations from the gravy train of European Union?

The reason I was speeding, officer, is that there was this car with flashing lights chasing me.

The reason that my velocity was in excess of the limitation indicated by the signage appertaining to this tarmacadam thoroughfare, constable, is that I was disturbed in my relaxed, inebriated journeying by a motor vehicle behind me with a display of distasteful coloured lights shining with rapid intermittence, and I felt I simply had to get away from such vulgarity.

LAW AND ORDER

I studied for the bar for three years, you know. So that's two pints of lager and a lemonade for the lady, right?

I spent three long years in academic amelioration for the bar, a fact which is now part of your knowledge. Heigh-ho and tinkerty-tonk, you were desirous that I should pour for you two imperial units of weak, pissy Euro-beer and a fizzy, sugary compound containing no lemon ingredients whatsoever despite its misleading nomenclature for your female escort, is that of a correctness?

AGE

I age like a fine wine: it's getting increasingly hard to pop my cork.

I ripen and mature rather in the manner of an exemplary beverage of fermented grape juice: the ejaculatory release of my wood is an increasingly bothersome challenge.

It's hard enough being my age, let alone acting it.

I suffer sufficiently from the challenge of merely existing at this stage in my life-cycle, and to be under an obligation to behave in a manner appropriate thereto would be an excessive nigglement.

Old people become a nuisance: they should be put down at birth.

Superannuated personages become exasperating nudnicks: they should be extirpated at the moment of their nascency.

www.summersdale.com